LIVING
WABI SABI

LIVING
WABI SABI

*The True Beauty
of Your Life*

TARO GOLD

**Andrews McMeel
Publishing**

Kansas City

*With appreciation
for my father,
who taught me where
the most beautiful
lotus flowers bloom.*

ISBN-13: 978-0-7407-3960-6
ISBN-10: 0-7407-3960-3

Library of Congress Control Number: 2004101335

05 06 07 08 TWP 10 9 8 7 6 5 4 3 2

Illustrations by Matthew Taylor
Book design by Lisa Martin

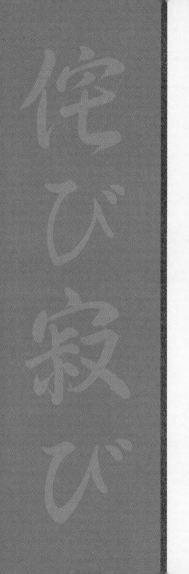

CONTENTS

A PERSONAL
INTRODUCTION

Seek always to progress

rather than to perfect.

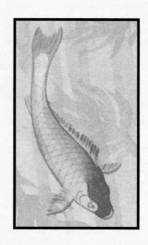

You and I have at least one thing in common: We're not perfect. And you know what? That's precisely how we're meant to be.

You and I are reflections of the perfectly imperfect nature of life itself. Once we make peace with ourselves, imperfections and all, we see that every ounce of success, love, and serenity we can imagine is our very birthright and the birthright of everyone around us.

Those who inspire us most do not achieve perfection through greatness: They achieve greatness through imperfection. All of the world's best-loved truth-seekers and religious figures, including Jesus and Buddha, led obviously less-than-perfect lives and were the first to let us know that they, too, were not perfect people. Today, however, it seems we are moving further away from this commonsense awareness.

My life in this wonderfully imperfect world began in California at the dawn of the 1970s, amid an eclectic mix of privilege and adversity. In childhood, I enjoyed acting in television commercials, modeling sportswear, doing voice-overs for Disney movies, and starring in Broadway musicals such as *Peter Pan*. I was my parents' only child and glad to be—attending the best private academies and vacationing in dozens of countries around the world with my two best friends, my mom and dad. From the outside, my life looked perfect.

On the inside, however, my parents struggled to maintain their marriage, my father battled with bipolar disorder, my mother and I suffered from chronic respiratory illnesses, my family endured a financial debacle that pushed us to the brink of homelessness, my neck was broken in a car accident with a drunk driver, and just after I was elected freshman class president in high school, my father suddenly died. My life was definitely imperfect, to say the least.

And yet, I wouldn't change a thing. Every hardship prompted inner journeys, leading me ultimately to greater joy and purpose than I thought possible. By embracing my life in its entirety—joys, triumphs, flaws, bungles, and disasters included—I came to see that trying to improve life and trying to perfect life, while they may seem one and the same, actually have opposite results. The wish to improve life is real and attainable, but the desire for a perfect life—the perfect home, the perfect health, the perfect job, the perfect love, whatever it is—is the desire for something nonexistent.

Unfortunately, the hard-to-escape barrage of "perfect" images in the media would have us believe otherwise. We all know the marketing mythology: Buy this perfect product, get that perfect life. Unattainable ideals are everywhere we turn: television, movies, books, magazines, songs. It's no wonder that notions of perfection sneak into our fantasies and appear in our scandalously selective memories. It's no wonder that, at times, we may feel we just aren't good enough, no matter how hard we try.

*T*his is the very perfection of a man,

to find out his own imperfection.

— SAINT AUGUSTINE

*R*ing the bells that still can ring.

Forget your perfect offering.

There is a crack, a crack in everything.

That's how the light gets in.

— LEONARD COHEN

The truth is that we are already perfect as we are: perfectly imperfect, that is. For all the positives in our lives, we will always have negatives, too. It's a delicate balancing act: Without the negatives in life, the positives will lose their value.

If we never again shed tears of pain, what would our laughter mean? How would a blue sky seem if we knew no rain? Who would each of us be without our idiosyncrasies? As I write this with my rambunctious Italian greyhound at my feet, I think, would she be as cute without that little crook in her wagging tail?

In the old days, the finest and most expensive Persian rugs were deliberately marred to add texture and allure. Ancient architects left the tops off their pyramids. The "unconquerable" hero Achilles had a vulnerable spot in his heel. Even the Liberty Bell has a spectacular crack down its side, which only adds to its meaning and appeal.

With all the good we encounter in life, there will always be at least a bit of bad, just as we will always find a piece of fortune in misfortune when we look close enough. Why does the Universe work in this mysterious way? Maybe because flaws and mishaps are great stimuli for growth and creativity.

Did you know that numerous imperfections, failures, and mistakes led to the discovery of DNA, penicillin, aspirin, X-rays, Teflon, Velcro, nylon, cornflakes, Coca-Cola, and chocolate chip cookies? In our own lives, it's not the parties and vacations but the mind-opening trials of heart and soul that lead us to our greatest personal discoveries.

This book celebrates just such discoveries. It's a journey that uncovers the joy, creativity, and empowerment of imperfection through a simple and ancient way of looking at life: the way of Wabi Sabi. From the commonsense insights of Wabi Sabi, we learn that it's not despite our problems but because of them that our hearts hold everything we need to be joyful. We come to see that where we want to go in life is forever found right where we are.

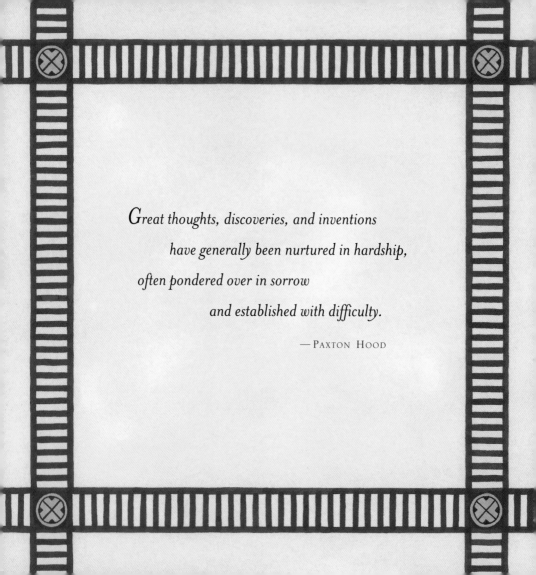

Great thoughts, discoveries, and inventions

have generally been nurtured in hardship,

often pondered over in sorrow

and established with difficulty.

— PAXTON HOOD

Only the idea of something is perfect.

    Its expression in material, worldly terms

is a mere shadow of that idea.

— PLATO

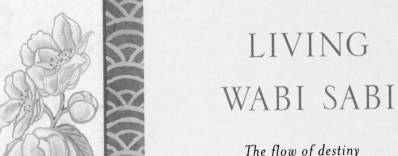

CHAPTER ONE

LIVING

WABI SABI

The flow of destiny

is yours to change.

人生

"You will grow to be even happier than you can possibly imagine today. And you will have all that your heart genuinely desires. You may not believe me now, but it's true. Do you want to know how this can be?"

I nodded from across the time-worn table upon which Obaa-san ("Grandmother" in Japanese) served me her famously delicious summer tea. My father had died just a few months before, and being an angst-filled teenager, I had come to soak up Obaa-san's reliable comfort and wisdom.

Perhaps Japanese tea, like blood, is thicker than water; for although we had no blood between us, Obaa-san was as much a grandmother to me as my own. She was a master of the Japanese tea ceremony, a trusted leader in the Buddhist community, and one of the most compassionate and enlightened people I've ever known. She taught me many things before my father died. Little did I know that she, like all fine teachers, had reserved her most valuable lessons for last.

Obaa-san sipped her tea and turned to me. "Why don't you join me tomorrow morning in the *butsuma*? We can pray together for your father and then have a good talk. I'll start *daimoku* at 7:00 A.M."

Obaa-san had never before invited me to the *butsuma*, a refined meditation-style room she used only for Buddhist study and *daimoku*, or chanting *Nam-myoho-renge-kyo*. The invitation took me by surprise, because she knew I balked at chanting. More than once before I had mocked her and my other relatives for their tea ceremonies, their chanting, and anything else I found arcane. Today was different. Maybe I was becoming an adult; maybe it was my father's passing. Whatever it was, I knew a heartfelt gift had been offered. I accepted.

The remainder of the evening found me lounging around

Obaa-san's comfortable estate.
Quaint by Western standards, to me
the traditional structure resembled
a small palace straight out of some
timeless Asian legend. It was a

majestic compound, built more than a hundred years earlier
in the lush countryside near Kyoto, the cultural and spiritual
heart of Japan. In its overgrown gardens, weather-beaten
stone lanterns stood guard beneath the sheltering arms of
oaks that must have already been old when the house was built.
It was a remnant of what I consider the true Japan.

In such a place, you can't help feeling the legacy of a grand
old civilization with all its dignity, beauty, and experience.
Even the sweltering humidity of the Kyoto summer only adds
to its richness. It was in this exceptional yet everyday setting,
in a place my schoolmates back home in California didn't
even know existed, that the lost gateway of living Wabi Sabi
opened before me.

Separated from today by oceans of time, the essence of a time-honored Japanese tradition known as Wabi Sabi is only vaguely understood by most Japanese people these days. If you ask people on a Tokyo street to describe it, they will likely give you a polite shrug and explain that Wabi Sabi is simply unexplainable. It is always "in the air"—few can put their finger on it.

By my teens, I had traveled around the world and lived for the most part in Southern California, so it was no surprise that I had even less understanding of Wabi Sabi than did my Japanese counterparts. Thanks to Obaa-san and others, however, the ancient wisdom of Asia never felt distant to me. No matter how unexciting I pretended it was, I quietly believed it was a treasure chest just waiting to be unlocked. I simply hadn't found my key. That is, until this extraordinary time in Kyoto.

This book holds many of the truths Obaa-san shared with me so patiently that summer. It is the path of discovery to a subtle yet powerful way of living: Living Wabi Sabi.

The art of living lies less in eliminating
our troubles than in growing with them.

— BERNARD M. BARUCH

Most folks are about as happy
as they make up their minds to be.

— ABRAHAM LINCOLN

Mistakes are the portals of discovery.

— JAMES JOYCE

CHAPTER TWO

LIKE SUGAR
FROM
THE SUN

The way of Wabi Sabi honors the quirks,

the oddities, the humble,

the unconventional. . . .

It celebrates the perfectly imperfect

uniqueness of you and me

and everything.

中道

We had just concluded our first chanting session together in her peaceful *butsuma*, and Obaa-san was aglow. "Life is perfectly imperfect," she said. "When you embrace the whole of your life and recognize the value of every aspect, including the mishaps and flaws, then the very imperfections that once diminished your happiness can become sources of insight and strength." Obaa-san smiled with the penetrating warmth and sweetness I always associate with her.

Her cool conviction was refreshing and contagious. It filled the room. I had to find out how a woman who had outlived most of her loved ones and suffered through war, famine, and disease could exude such a powerful life force.

When she was not much older than I, the tempest of war had destroyed nearly everything she had ever known. I could only gaze in admiration now at the fulfillment, the tranquillity, the joy and confidence that emanated from the woman in front of me. How, I wondered, could I get from where I was to where Obaa-san sat? My search for answers began that day with my introduction to the ancient ways of living Wabi Sabi.

"Wabi Sabi shares its history and development with certain customs and forms of Japanese Buddhism," Obaa-san said. "Wabi Sabi itself, however, is not a religion or even a Buddhist concept. From the spiritual perspective, Wabi Sabi is a universal ideal that can be easily adapted to any religious or philosophical background.

"A key aspect of living Wabi Sabi is individuality and uniqueness. Practice whatever religion or philosophy best suits you, or practice no religion at all, and Wabi Sabi can still enhance your life."

For most of her life, Obaa-san had practiced Nichiren Buddhism in the Soka Gakkai tradition. "At a young age," Obaa-san recounted, "I decided the most important thing was to develop my inner character and contribute goodness to the world. After exploring many philosophies, I discovered that my personal values were reflected most accurately in Nichiren Buddhism, and so I chose this path as my own. Whatever path you choose," she smiled, "follow it with all your heart."

"But what about Wabi Sabi?" I asked. "If it's not a religion, then how does it fit in with people like you who practice a particular philosophy, such as Christianity, Judaism, or Buddhism?"

"Wabi Sabi is simple," Obaa-san said. "Anyone can benefit from the ideals of Wabi Sabi, just as any kind of fruit becomes sweeter from the rays of the sun. The sun doesn't add sugar; the sugar is already in the fruit. The sun only helps reveal it. In this way, your philosophy of life is like the fruit, and Wabi Sabi is like the sun making sweeter what was already there."

How poetic and succinct. Now my curiosity was piqued. I wanted to know everything Obaa-san knew about Wabi Sabi. Each morning and night for the next few weeks, Obaa-san and I shared some tea while she illuminated the lost path of living Wabi Sabi.

We all live with the objective of being happy;

our lives are all different,

and yet the same.

—ANNE FRANK

The person who has never made a mistake

will never make anything else.

—GEORGE BERNARD SHAW

Even if you've never heard of Wabi Sabi, it's surprisingly easy to understand, because you and everyone you have ever known are living examples of it—as is everything in the Universe. In a nutshell, Wabi Sabi is imperfection, or more fully, appreciation of the value and beauty of imperfection. Wabi Sabi celebrates the preciousness of all things imperfect, which is truly *all* things.

The way of Wabi Sabi honors the quirks, the oddities, the perfectly imperfect uniqueness of you and me and everything. Wabi Sabi highlights the value of objects, events, and the entirety of your life "as is," unpolished, unpredictable, and natural.

"For at least the past five hundred years or so," Obaa-san said, "Wabi Sabi has been closely linked with the Japanese tea ceremony." A pillar of Japanese cultural heritage, the tea ceremony is a refined art (performance art, really) that is studied and practiced over the course of years or even a lifetime. As with many cultural schools of art in Asia, certain families are well known in their respective fields.

Since Obaa-san was raised in just such a family, one with a proud lineage of Tea Masters, her awareness of the tea ceremony and of all things Wabi Sabi was virtually inborn.

For those of us raised in the West, the title "Tea Master" may have an amusing ring. This is not the case in Asia, and particularly in Japan, where Tea Masters have for centuries been highly regarded teachers and leaders. Powerful families of Tea Masters controlled the flow of cultural information and "intellectual property," including concepts like Wabi Sabi. Huge sums were charged for cultural lessons and related merchandise, including items used in tea ceremonies. This system created enormous wealth for some families but also stifled the free transmission of cultural heritage from one generation to the next.

"As a result," Obaa-san lamented, "the wisdom of Wabi Sabi became more mysterious and obscure. Fewer and fewer people over the centuries came to comprehend its full meaning. By the modern era, its original spirit was all but scattered into near extinction."

Wabi Sabi encourages balance
throughout every aspect of life.
Our spiritual experiences are Wabi. . . .
The material aspects of our lives are Sabi.

Wabi Sabi celebrates the beauty and allure of imperfection:
the cozy familiarity of a worn-out pair of jeans,
the rustic elegance of an old Italian villa,
the faded splendor of well-used china
handed down from your grandmother's attic.

Wabi Sabi expresses universal sensibility. . . .
Its messages can be easily adapted to
any religious or cultural background.

So what is Wabi Sabi? In English there exists no single word or phrase to accurately express the whole of it. Wabi Sabi is simultaneously a narrow path and a wide boulevard. In the narrow view, Wabi Sabi fosters a bohemian sense of beauty that celebrates the basic, the unique, and the imperfect. In the wider sense, Wabi Sabi is a worldview that supports ecocentric living and compassionate humanism. Perhaps the truest form of Wabi Sabi is found somewhere between these two paths—the middle way, as it were.

The Chinese characters used to write "Wabi Sabi" originated more than three thousand years ago. The character for *Wabi* represents the inner, or spiritual, experiences of our lives. Its original meaning indicated an "empty," "lonely," or "basic" state. The character for *Sabi* represents the outer, or material, aspects of life. Originally, it meant "worn," "weathered," or "decayed."

Together, these downtrodden images reflect the harsh living conditions many people faced daily throughout

Japanese history. Westerners are often surprised to learn that, in contrast to its wealth today, the nation of Japan was unable to consistently feed and care for its people until the twentieth century. Japan is an island nation that has historically suffered from a chronic lack of natural resources, a harsh climate (including typhoons and floods), sporadic earthquakes, volcanoes, fires, wars, tsunami, plagues, and famine.

With these adverse circumstances as a backdrop, and after centuries of incorporating artistic and Buddhist influences from China, Wabi Sabi eventually evolved into a distinctly Japanese ideal. Over time, the meanings of both words (*Wabi* and *Sabi*) shifted to become more lighthearted and hopeful. Around seven hundred years ago, the humble Wabi Sabi images of "emptiness" and "imperfection" began to take on a distinctly more enlightened tone.

Particularly among the nobility, understanding emptiness was considered the most effective means to spiritual awakening (as we will see in Chapter 5), while embracing imperfection was honored as a healthy reminder to cherish our unpolished selves, here and now, just as we are—the first step to *satori,* or enlightenment.

In today's Japan, the meaning of *Wabi Sabi* is often condensed to "wisdom in natural simplicity." In art books, it is typically defined as "flawed beauty."

Obaa-san explained how Wabi Sabi's forgiving standard of beauty evolved through its integration in the Japanese tea ceremony. Intentionally imperfect tea-related objects were created to fit the Wabi Sabi ideal and, unlike the extravagance of those in China, the tea houses of Japan emphasized simplicity and a return to more rustic designs. Ecocentric Wabi Sabi designers strove to dissolve their tea houses into the surrounding gardens and native landscape to promote a greater appreciation for the natural environment. This is also where the notion of Zen gardening as a spiritual practice began.

"I could go on, but you know enough about the past now," Obaa-san said. "It's what we do today with our knowledge of the past that matters. I want you to see how to apply Wabi Sabi here and now. I want you to know how living Wabi Sabi can transform your life, now and in the future. Like sugar from the sun."

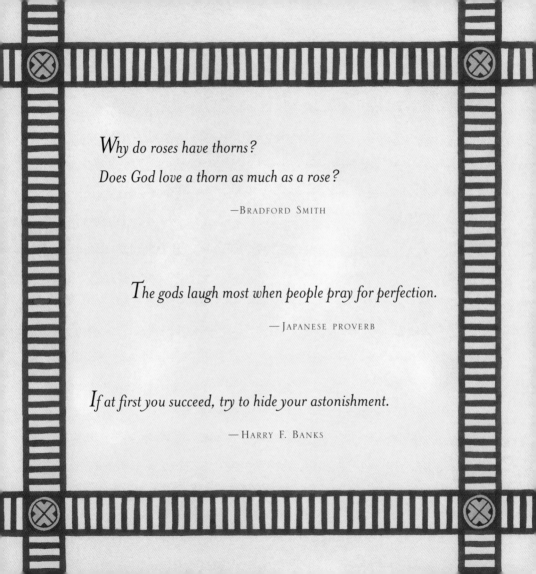

Why do roses have thorns?

Does God love a thorn as much as a rose?

—Bradford Smith

The gods laugh most when people pray for perfection.

— Japanese proverb

If at first you succeed, try to hide your astonishment.

— Harry F. Banks

CHAPTER THREE

THE WISDOM
OF
IMPERFECTION

Looking through the eyes of Wabi Sabi,
we see the beauty and value of
life's imperfect parts
and the hidden treasures they reveal.

智

恵

"Someday in the future, I hope the wisdom of Wabi Sabi, the wisdom of imperfection, will be seen as common sense. That's what it is, really, common sense. No matter our religious or cultural heritage, living Wabi Sabi can help us become more joyful." And with that, Obaa-san turned our conversation to the topic of joy.

"Everyone wants to be joyful, yet everyone faces some worry or another. We all encounter loss, challenge, hardship, even disaster in the course of our lives. Whether our difficulties are internal or external, minor or major, changeable or unchangeable, problems are an inherent part of life. We can use these problems, these 'imperfections,' to enrich our lives, to help us determine priorities and goals, and to become the person we want to be. For most people, this is a difficult attitude adjustment."

Obaa-san's words brought to mind a friend, Samantha. Sam once broke her leg in a bizarre accident involving a cardboard box and a French poodle. (I never understood the details.) Sam ended up in the hospital overnight, lamenting her woes. The worst part was that she had been training for months to run a marathon the following week. "All that effort wasted," she cried.

Sam made a choice. "I could have just climbed under a rock, drowning in self-pity—and, believe me, that was very appealing," she later told me. "Or I could look for the rainbow in the rainstorm." And that's what she did. When the marathon was under way, Sam was standing on the sidelines cheering on her fellow runners.

Since she was in such outstanding emotional and physical condition, Sam's recovery was remarkable. One doctor was more than impressed: He fell in love and later became her husband. "Breaking my leg was the best thing that ever happened to me," Sam said. "I met my partner, plus I realized how much I enjoy running and helping other athletes perform better." Today, Sam is a successful track coach with a special appreciation for the twists and turns of life.

Appreciation—emotional appreciation, artistic appreciation, appreciation on every level—is an important part of living Wabi Sabi.

Appreciation manifests joy. We don't need to live by some impossible standard to have a joyful, contributive, "enlightened" existence. We don't need to become someone else or wait until things are "perfect" to appreciate the whole of our lives.

Television, movies, and romance novels often paint a very different picture of joy—a "happily ever after" that includes no wrinkles, no chips, no stumbles. But that's not reality.

"We are all looking for joy . . . every day . . . always . . . this way or that," Obaa-san said. "I've traveled the world teaching the art of tea, and in all the countries I've visited, the people I befriend express the same wish time and again— to know joy. No matter how we define it—achievement, wealth, family, health—our desire for joy guides our actions and colors our perspectives. Entire libraries of ponderous books analyze this desire in excruciating detail."

"Yes," I said. "One of my teachers told me that humanity's greatest thinkers from East to West, like Confucius and Aristotle, have always believed that joy is the ultimate goal of all people. Our search for joy has been the same for thousands of years."

"People often fantasize that lasting joy will come to them as a result of perfection," Obaa-san continued. "Most people dream of the perfect mate, the perfect job, the perfect home, and so on. But to wish for perfection is to deny reality. It actually invites the opposite of what we seek.

Perfection exists only in the imagination. As long as we equate joy with perfection in even a small way, we will never know contentment.

"The ancient Wabi Sabi masters understood this well," she said. "They knew that happiness does not mean 'absence of problems.' There has never been, nor will there ever be, a life free from problems. Since there is no such thing as a perfect life, Wabi Sabi teaches us a way of looking at life that accepts imperfections, makes peace with the difficulties and mishaps, and strives to use them for our ultimate enrichment."

As we continued to sip our tea, I absorbed Obaa-san's words. I realized that imperfections in life take a multitude of forms. There are as many types of imperfections as there are people on Earth, yet all imperfections share one thing:

the potential to cause suffering or, at best, discomfort. Perhaps for this reason, we imagine that perfection will bring us comfort and joy. But this is an illusion.

After a moment of silence, I said, "It's like the Japanese proverb: 'There is always a piece of fortune in misfortune.'"

"Yes." Obaa-san nodded. "That's absolutely correct. We can find good within bad in any situation. The trick is to unlearn what we have been taught about the relationship between joy and imperfection, to shift our perspective."

One does not discard gold

    because the bag holding it is dirty . . .

One does not refuse to gather lotuses

    because the water in which they grow is unclean.

— NICHIREN

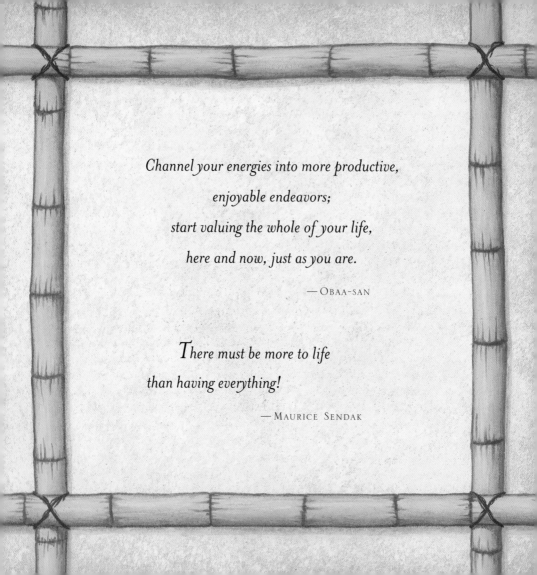

Channel your energies into more productive,

enjoyable endeavors;

start valuing the whole of your life,

here and now, just as you are.

— Obaa-san

There must be more to life

than having everything!

— Maurice Sendak

"Deep in your heart, you have always known the truths of living Wabi Sabi," Obaa-san said as she calmly poured another cup of tea. "I'm simply here to remind you of those quiet truths, to counterbalance the years of other voices that have drowned them out. From one direction or another, you have learned to hide, ignore, or resist the imperfections in your life and your surroundings, and you've probably done it well. Most everyone has. Now the time has come to channel that energy into more productive, enjoyable endeavors, to start valuing the whole of your life. Rather than defeat the imperfections in life, living Wabi Sabi will help you to redefine the negatives, to understand their hidden, positive lessons and become a more joyful person along the way."

Over the years, I have come to understand Obaa-san's words on increasingly deeper levels. We are not perfect. We are not supposed to be perfect. We simply are.

When we cherish ourselves as we are, we accept other

people and things as they are. We come to show more compassion, patience, and thoughtfulness. We bring more humor and lightness to any situation. When we broaden our attitude to embrace everything as perfectly imperfect, we begin to see more clearly what's truly important to us, and we increase our joy of living.

In my life, I've visited with orphans in the slums of India and idled with superstars in French palaces. I'm not going to pretend that Paris isn't more fun than Calcutta. But what my experiences have proven to me is that the trappings of a so-called perfect life—money, fame, status, and so on—do not make you happy. *You* make you happy.

Material wealth can be useful, even pleasant, but it is irrelevant to joy. At the end of the day, it doesn't really matter what you have or don't have, because joy comes from within—it is untouched by outside circumstances.

Unlike happiness, which comes and goes with every up and down in life, joy is absolute. You may be unhappy for whatever reason, but you can still feel joy under any condition.

The desperately poor children I met in Calcutta are living proof of the unshakable nature of joy. The only homes they had ever known were the filthy streets of the city. In hundred-degree heat, they played on rotting piles of garbage as gleefully as if they were in paradise. They could hardly scrounge enough for themselves to survive, yet they kept a small dog as their beloved pet, sharing with her what tidbits they had, teetering on the edge of life together, smiling all the way. Those children radiated more spontaneous joy than most people I know who live in sprawling luxury.

From the mansions of Bel Air to the shanties of Soweto, one thing is certain: We must each find our own unique recipe for a joyful life. There exists no cookie-cutter pattern to follow, no standard mix of ingredients, regardless of who or where we are. Life isn't this way or that. Life simply is.

Children know this truth instinctively. Until someone teaches them differently, children pay no mind to arbitrary value judgments. Children see possibility where others see nothing. Children know that an empty canvas is the best kind, because you can paint whatever you want on it.

In Miami, Bangkok, Buenos Aires, or Tel Aviv, give children nothing more than sand and they will build a castle. That's the magic of life to a child. There is endless potential everywhere.

Life is always that way. It can be that way for us, too—but sometimes we forget.

"Do you remember who you were as a child?" Obaa-san asked with a caring tone. "Who you were as a child is the most Wabi Sabi part of you. It is the most important part of you.

"Who you were as a child is your true self—not the person who others want you to be or who you *think* they want you to be but the person you are. That's your unique spirit—the part that can keep you forever joyful and free and creative—the fountainhead of youthfulness. Always remember who you were as a child, my dear."

As Obaa-san and I reminisced about my early years, I saw how very Wabi Sabi I had been as a child, blissfully singing off-key, happily running and bumping into things, mispronouncing words with gusto, and drawing outside the lines just because I could.

Children find no shame in being real. They thrive on the Wabi Sabi-ness of themselves and everything around them and often wear it on their sleeves for the whole world to see. Left to their own devices, children are not afraid of being whoever they truly are—at least not until someone teaches them otherwise.

As a kid, I had to learn (often the hard way) to hide some things I enjoyed (art, music, dance) as they were social death knells in the world of boys. When it came to things I couldn't hide, such as "throwing like a girl" (a classic pariah-maker), I had a choice: get a new throwing arm or stop throwing. I elected to evade, at all costs, sports that involved throwing and successfully took up surfing and soccer instead.

A written list of this and all the Wabi Sabi moments in just one childhood could span halfway across the ocean. Add this to the potentially limitless Wabi Sabi experiences of our private worlds—personal thoughts, difficult family

lives, social problems, health problems, and so on—and the list could easily reach the moon.

None of these myriad Wabi-Sabi aspects of our lives are sources of embarrassment until we learn from others that they are. At some point, we are taught that these normal aspects of our lives are faults—shameful, mistaken, less than acceptable, out of line, not quite perfect. Regrettably, many of us are taught early on to be uncomfortable with the differences in our lives, to make sure we always color inside the lines that other people have drawn. Few of us are taught to use imperfections for our betterment, to seek the hidden lesson that every difficulty holds, to be proud of our uniqueness.

Over time, we may discover that denying or hiding parts of our lives (from both ourselves and others) requires enormous time and energy and can be terribly unhealthy.

Contentment begins with acceptance. We must look

our idiosyncrasies and imperfections squarely in the face to begin their transformation into empowerment. With a dose of patience and humor, we can find surprising new ways of accentuating our strengths by exploring and understanding our weaknesses. Ironically, our worst imperfections and setbacks often lead us to our most spectacular developments, talents, and personal achievements.

Babe Ruth struck out twice as often as he hit home runs. Albert Einstein failed his college entrance exam; teachers described him as "mentally slow, and adrift in foolish dreams." Agatha Christie couldn't spell; she had to dictate her mysteries. A young Walt Disney was fired from his first media job for "lack of imagination." Michael Jordan was cut from his high school basketball team.

"Depending on how we take them, failures, imperfections, and adversity can be great sources of motivation and opportunity," Obaa-san said. "Sometimes we feel deep frustration, anger, or sadness due to our struggles. This is natural. Rather than escape or reject unpleasant circumstances, however, we should follow our feelings to the true origin of our suffering so that we can transform it into a source of benefit and triumph."

"Hmmm," I replied after some consideration. "I think I'd prefer to keep rejecting imperfections and unpleasantness. Transforming them sounds like too much work!" We both had a good laugh.

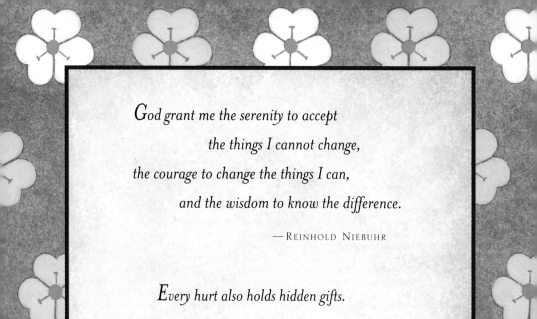

*G*od grant me the serenity to accept

　　　　the things I cannot change,

the courage to change the things I can,

　　　　and the wisdom to know the difference.

— REINHOLD NIEBUHR

*E*very hurt also holds hidden gifts.

— OBAA-SAN

*R*emember this—very little is needed to make a joyful life.
It is all in your way of thinking.

— MARCUS AURELIUS

"But seriously," I asked, "what's wrong, for example, with leaving a job or ending a relationship when it causes us grief?"

Obaa-san grinned. "Well, depending on the situation, perhaps you *should* quit a bad job or break up with a difficult mate, but don't expect that to increase your sense of joy. Without understanding how your choices led to where you stand, you are apt to repeat the same mistakes. Switching environments helps only when you first make a switch in yourself. To put it in theatrical terms, 'Changing scenery does not change the script.'"

Obaa-san paused, gazing out the window. As a gentle breeze rustled through the trees, a wind chime rang out in the distance. The quiet melody faded, and she continued.

"Believe it or not," Obaa-san said, "no matter how it may seem at the time, the core of your suffering is *not* your inconsiderate partner, your demanding boss, your insufficient bank balance, or whatever. The root of your suffering is found internally, in the limitations you place on yourself.

"With every painful situation we face in life, we receive an opportunity, a chance to break through our boundaries and expand our potential. Every upsetting emotion, from the most trivial nuisance to the most agonizing heartache, originates from within ourselves. Therefore, we are in command of our suffering. If we can feel it inside ourselves, then we also have the power within to transform it."

Obaa-san excused herself while she retrieved a book from her study. She returned carrying a fine, hand-tooled journal. "I collect in this book," she said, placing it carefully on the table between us, "precious words of wisdom from friends, mentors, and sages of old." She opened the cover to reveal waves of flowing calligraphy on each delicate page. With a twinkle in her eye, she smiled and announced, "I've even included a few gems that you've shared with me over the years!"

"Really?" I asked, as she turned the pages with increasing speed, as if to find proof. "But I'm too young!"

Obaa-san looked up and, breaking into another smile, said, "Truth is truth and wisdom is wisdom, regardless of the source. Age has nothing to do with it, my dear.

"The great philosophers, both East and West, may have been older than you when people first took notice of them, but they were born wise. Just like you. Just like all of us. Everyone holds the same wisdom in their hearts—some people simply find ways of tapping into theirs more readily than others. Knowledge changes with age, yes, because information is of the past. Wisdom and truth, however, are constant; they are timeless.

"Speaking of truth and wisdom," Obaa-san continued, "I want to show you something here in my journal. Anytime you feel frustrated, this passage will help you."

In striking Japanese calligraphy along the page's edge were the words "Guidance of the honorable Josei Toda,

second president of the Soka Gakkai Buddhist association."
Meticulously inscribed, it read:

> When we are upset, it's easy to blame others. The
> true cause of our feelings, however, is within us.
> For example, imagine yourself as a glass of water.
> Now, imagine past negative experiences as sediment
> at the bottom of your glass. Next, think of an
> unpleasant situation as a spoon. When the spoon
> stirs, the sediment clouds your water. It may
> appear that the spoon caused the water to cloud—
> but if there were no sediment, the water would
> remain clear. Even if we remove the spoon, our
> sediment still remains—lying in wait for the next
> spoon to appear. On the other hand, if we remove
> our sediment, then no matter how a spoon may
> stir, our water will remain clear.

"This is powerful insight," Obaa-san said. "Heed these golden words whenever you feel distressed. By carrying this illumination in your heart, you can see every stormy circumstance or emotion for what it truly is—an opening for you to increase your clarity and expand your joy. This is the wisdom of imperfection."

Experience is what we call

the accumulation of our mistakes.

— Yiddish proverb

We do not attract that which we want,

we attract that which we are.

— James Allen

If you want your future to be different
than your past, study your past.

— Baruch Spinoza

CHAPTER FOUR

GROWING UP, GROWING DOWN

Once you can feel the greatness
of little things inside yourself,
you will feel the littleness
of great things outside yourself.

成長

*I*t was morning again, and new sunlight streamed into Obaa-san's *butsuma*. I was not used to rising with the sun, at least not during summer vacation, but this had been Obaa-san's daily ritual for more than half a century. Now, it was becoming mine as well.

After an hour or so of chanting, which seemed at once momentary and eternal, we turned to face each other. Obaa-san's cheerful eyes glowed with a light as beautiful as the tiny rainbows cast by crystal lotus flowers adorning her Buddhist altar. Each morning, the crystal caught stray beams of the rising sun, transforming them into a light show. It struck me that just as those crystal flowers lit up

Obaa-san's exterior space, so did her daily practice of chanting *Nam-myoho-renge-kyo* illuminate her inner space.

This was the remarkable yet ordinary setting in which Obaa-san introduced me to the wider message of Wabi Sabi, which is more than just an appreciation of imperfection. Wabi Sabi encompasses the oneness of ourselves and our environment, a deep conviction in the law of cause and effect (karma), a cherishing of our essential selves, and much, much more.

As Obaa-san and I settled in to share some tea, as had become our custom after chanting, she posed a question. "What would you call everything from your skin inward?" she asked. "Probably your 'self,' yes?"

"Of course," I replied.

"And what would you call everything from your skin outward? Probably your 'environment' or 'surroundings.' People generally see the world in this way, divided into two realms—self and surroundings. If you look closely, however, you will see that these two realms are actually one. The whole world is, in fact, an extension of your body.

"In my journal I keep a quote from the great British poet John Donne that reads 'No man is an Island.' This is absolutely true. Although islands may appear to be separated by vast stretches of water, deep beneath the surface they are all connected to the same earth. Likewise, you may think of yourself and your surroundings as separate, yet in the ultimate reality, you and your surroundings are completely intertwined."

At first, this concept did not seem like an earth-shattering revelation. I found, however, that developing a deep awareness of it proved empowering beyond expectation.

Why is this concept so powerful? Because it explains that, regardless of past experience and current circumstances, you have the ability to create, develop, mold, and improve your situation, your relationships, and anything else in your daily life through your own inner reformation.

"It's like the relationship between you and your room," Obaa-san said. "Look at your room. What does it look like today? What does it look like almost every day? Whenever I've seen it, since you were a little boy, it's been messy, with papers and books and clothes and all sorts of things strewn about."

"Yep, that's my room all right," I had to admit.

"Have you seen your cousin Alexandra's room? It's also full of things, but it's organized; nothing is ever out of place. Then there's her brother's room, which is neither organized nor messy—it's open and simple. Whatever the case, your room is in many ways a reflection of you, and vice versa. Although you and your room are separate entities, you are dependent upon each other. You can affect the room's condition, and the room's condition— whether clean or dirty, too cold, too hot, or just right— can affect yours.

"In the same way, our greater surroundings, such as work, school, family, and our natural environment, compose the rooms of our lives. We can allow them to contain us and influence our condition, or we can choose to contain them and influence their condition. The difference lies solely in our choice of direction: growing up, or growing down."

Growing up? Growing down? I raised a quizzical brow.

*Like a mirror reflecting
whatever stands before it,
the reality of our outer world
reflects the condition of our inner world.*

*The direction of our actions
creates the direction of our lives.
The direction of our lives
creates the direction of our world.*

"Regardless of age," Obaa-san continued, "there are two ways of growing. We either proactively grow up, or we habitually grow down.

"When we feel a strong sense of self, confident of our worth regardless of external circumstances; when we take responsibility for our choices, living a creative life, we continually grow up."

As newborns, we have no sense of ourselves as separate from everything around us. We see no distinctions. In that context, we are physically small yet spiritually immense. Infants are boundlessly united with the world.

As we continue to grow, we come to distinguish our body from other things, and we start to identify with a name that has been given to us. We recognize our image in a mirror and can see ourselves as others do, limited by our tiny physical appearance, yet we can still experience the infinity of our inner spiritual world. Maintaining this balance between our outer limited form and our inner limitless self is essential to growing up.

Obaa-san continued with an explanation of "growing down." "When we've lost our way," she said, "unsure of our innate power and potential, swayed by external circumstances; when we fail to take responsibility for our choices, living a life of habit, we grow down.

"Occasionally, as we mature, we lose the balance between our expansive inner self and our limited outer self. Other people's view of us as a relatively tiny being in a massive Universe overruns our personal vision of endless self. Instead of our lives containing the world, the world begins to contain us. We are no longer whole; we are reduced to only a part of our true self. Just as the moon can overshadow the sun, our smaller identity moves to the fore, eclipsing the greater light of our inner self.

"More than anyone, people who have grown down need the wisdom of Wabi Sabi, yet they are the least likely to accept it. They can't hear it. They can't see it. They're too busy trying to camouflage their imperfections, battling as best they can each day to rein in their untamed insecurities. They're fighting a personal civil war, with no hope of a winner."

Obaa-san taught me to see that everything in life is connected. Our inner and our outer worlds are like the lines of a huge interwoven net. When we move one line of a net, every line moves. In this way, our inner world and outer world can affect each other. This interconnectedness gives us a choice. We can allow our environment to influence us, define us, mold us in its image, and we risk growing down. Or we can choose to shape our environment by first shaping ourselves, and we will grow up. The choice is ours; the power is completely within each of us.

Like a mirror reflecting whatever stands before it, the mirror of our surroundings—our relationships, our job, our home, and so on—reflects the reality of our inner world—

our desires, our emotions, our thoughts, and our spirituality. In other words, if what we see in our surroundings isn't all we want it to be, perhaps we've been growing down. When we continually focus on growing up, tapping the power of our limitless inner vision, our environment naturally changes to reflect this view.

"Revealing your inner gifts is not only for personal gain," Obaa-san emphasized. "The way of Wabi Sabi teaches that as you begin to manifest your full potential, everyone and everything around you will be positively affected as well. It's a matter of continually growing and of always growing up."

We are a strand in the web of life.
Whatever we do to the web, we do to ourselves.
All things are connected.

— CHIEF SEATTLE

Those who do not grow, grow smaller.

— RABBI HILLEL

Nature uses only the longest threads
to weave her patterns,
so each small piece of her fabric reveals
the organization of her entire tapestry.

— RICHARD FEYNMAN

*Mother Earth provides enough
to satisfy everyone's need,
but not enough for everyone's greed.*

— MAHATMA GANDHI

Obaa-san explained that as we consciously grow up, we naturally change for the better. In turn our world—both our personal circumstances and our natural environment—changes for the better. Honoring the well-being of both our personal and our natural environments is a core principle of living Wabi Sabi.

The Wabi Sabi masters of ancient Japan shared a great respect for nature. Even in the face of natural disasters, they admired the beauty and dignity of nature above all else.

Obaa-san's thoughts broke for a moment, distracted by the patter of an unexpected rain shower. As the heavens burst open, glistening sheets of water draped the house and gardens.

"The Earth is a single living being," Obaa-san continued. "Mother Earth is alive. She is her own shining sphere of life, floating in time and space. Her skin is transparent atmosphere; her bones are mountains and lands. Her

cells are you and me and every living creature within her boundaries. Her blood is water, her veins are rivers, her organs are oceans, her lungs are forests, and her breath is wind. As the parts resemble the whole, so are the similarities between our bodies and the body of Mother Earth."

From this view, if we understand that the health of each cell in our body contributes to our general health, then we can understand how the health of each living thing on Earth creates the general health of our planet. "When people go to war, it's like a cancer erupting in the body of Mother Earth," Obaa-san said. "And when we choose actions that damage our natural environment, we become like a virus eating away at the structure of Mother

Earth's body. In the vast net of life, everything is interwoven. It is for our own good that we should mend our ways."

In the years since I first heard those words, our world has borne witness to the consequences of ignoring our link to the vast net of life. Despite the best efforts of environmentalists, the level of poisonous gases that industries around the world pump into our atmosphere continues to rise. At the same time, our precious oxygen-giving forests are being chopped down at an increasing pace. Thirty years ago, one-fourth of Earth's land was covered by forests. Just ten years ago, that area had shrunk to one-fifth. Today, it has been reduced to only one-sixth.

Meanwhile, evidence of global warming continues to mount. Scientists studying the subject have become even more alarmed by recent events. Rhode Island-size chunks of ice are breaking off along a fast-warming edge of Antarctica that had been icebound for more than twelve thousand years.

These massive new icebergs completely disintegrate within a month, far sooner than anyone expected.

In tropical regions, coral reefs such as those near Australia are showing bleaching and other signs of death by human pollution. Living coral reefs are the foundation of marine life and thus critical support for human life.

Alaska and other northern areas are also being hit hard by climatic changes. Retreating sea ice has led to increasingly intense waves battering Alaska's coast, undermining villages that must relocate farther from the shoreline. Herds of sea creatures and animals, including walrus, whales, polar bears, and caribou, on which native inhabitants such as the Inuit depend for survival, are being devastated by warmer temperatures.

Just as our bodies become ill from internal irregularities, so can the body of Mother Earth fall ill from disruptions to her delicate balance. We can contribute to the pollution of our natural environment for only so long before we personally begin to feel the consequences, just as otherwise healthy cells will suffer in an ailing body.

It is never too late to make a change, however. As Obaa-san taught me, it's simple. Whether it's our personal surroundings at home, work, or school, or the broader concerns of Mother Earth, it's a matter of choice—of choosing direction.

The direction of our actions creates the direction of our lives. The direction of our lives creates the direction of our world. It's up to each of us which direction we will grow: up or down.

In the deeper reality beyond space and time,

we may be all members of one body.

—SIR JAMES JEANS

How wonderful it is

that nobody need wait

a single moment

before starting to improve the world.

—ANNE FRANK

*W*hat lies behind us

and what lies before us

are tiny matters compared to

what lies within us.

— WILLIAM MARAN

CHAPTER FIVE

AWAKENING TO THE UNIVERSE WITHIN

Life is the channeling of energy
from one form to another.
Our journey is without beginning,
as it is without end.
All emerge from, exist by,
and return to the Universe.

My time in Kyoto was flying by—two weeks had passed in what felt like only two days. As I set the table for dinner one evening in my last week there, I said to Obaa-san, "This Saturday will be my last day in Kyoto for who knows how long. Before I return to America, I want to know if there is anything you haven't already told me that you think I should know. Anything you think is important."

Obaa-san laughed. "Anything I think is important! Do you have another year to stay and listen? Instead, answer this question: What exactly do you want to know?"

A train of thoughts I'd been holding back sped through my mind. "How did the Wabi Sabi masters view the purpose of life? Where do we come from before we're born? What happens when we die? Does prayer make a difference? What is the ultimate truth of the Universe—from your perspective, from the Wabi Sabi perspective?"

Obaa-san dropped her jaw in feigned shock. "What easy questions! Just basic concerns teenagers lose sleep over, I suppose," she said, tongue in cheek. "Of course, those are actually some of the most profound uncertainties ever pondered. I'll be happy to share my thoughts with you, and I hope you will always look to yourself for answers as well."

I expected Obaa-san would use the remaining days in my visit to explain her ideas to me. To my surprise, she thoroughly answered all my questions before we finished dinner.

"There is an anthem of life," she began, "a harmony of Universal energy that permeates everything. It is the orchestration of pure freedom, joy, and creativity—the rhythmic energy of life itself. The more we align ourselves with this rhythmic energy, the more freedom, joy, and creativity flow through our lives.

"As an infinite ocean of creativity, the rhythmic energy of the Universe is the wellspring of potential that Mother Nature calls upon to shape our world and beyond.

"Did you know that the same energy particles and elements that compose our bodies also make up the vast celestial bodies of distant space? This is basic yet powerful information, for it tells us that we are one with the Universe—we contain the Universe, as the Universe contains us. We call upon the same energy to create thoughts in our minds as the Universe does to create stars in the heavens," Obaa-san said.

This essential energy of which Obaa-san spoke is familiar to us all. Depending on where and how we were raised, we may attempt to describe this indescribable reality as Jehovah, God, Allah, the Creator, or perhaps Truth, Brahma, Tao, or the Middle Way. Obaa-san used the collective term *Universe*. Whatever the expression, all refer to the same progressive force that gives rise to everything.

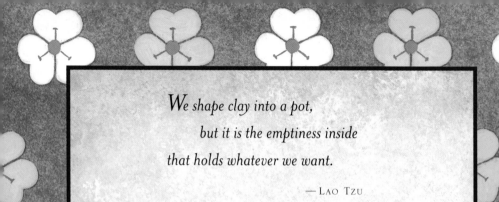

We shape clay into a pot,
    but it is the emptiness inside
that holds whatever we want.

— LAO TZU

When we align our intentions with those of the Universe,
    with the flow of life's rhythmic energy,
        our life naturally moves toward
            our noblest dreams.

— OBAA-SAN

It is only with the heart that one can see rightly.
What is essential is invisible to the eye.

— ANTOINE DE SAINT-EXUPÉRY

The first Wabi Sabi masters taught that "emptiness" is the ultimate reality of the Universe. Emptiness, as they saw it, is at the core of everything. This ancient wisdom has proven to be remarkably accurate. Quantum science tells us that the structures of atoms that compose our bodies (and our homes and the forests and all things) are, in fact, 99.999 percent empty. Everything in the material world, no matter how "solid" we think it to be, is proportionately as void as intergalactic space.

Buddhist scriptures informed the Wabi Sabi masters that this emptiness is filled with energy, and this energy gives rise to all existence. Since energy is eternal, they proposed, everything in the Universe must also be eternal. Although the ancient sages had no way of proving this, today we know that the amount of energy in the Universe is indeed constant, and that although energy can be channeled into different forms, it can never be created or destroyed. Energy simply is.

"From the viewpoint of Wabi Sabi," Obaa-san explained, "it is the hidden energy within emptiness that gives rise to all. Everyone and everything are constantly moving either toward or away from the state of emptiness. We can also think of this as moving between existence and nonexistence. In other words, life and death are not two states but different aspects of the same state."

"This reminds me," I interjected, "of the life cycle of stars. We studied this in school last semester. When a star in space dies and disappears from sight, its essence, its elemental energy, remains as an invisible residue. After some time, its basic elements merge once again, causing a new star to be born."

"Yes," Obaa-san agreed, "and just as that is true with outer space, so it is with inner space. In life, our physical self moves to the foreground while our spiritual self blends into the background. In death, it is the reverse—our spiritual self comes to the foreground while our physical self melds into the background."

Since I had taken up surfing a few years earlier (after my "throwing-like-a-girl" experiences), I thought of waves in the ocean. As waves are individual expressions of the ocean, so are we individual expressions of Universal energy. When a wave is born, we can see its physical form as it charges along, connected to but different from the ocean. When a wave dies, we can no longer see it, as its physical form returns fully to the ocean from where it came. We are as waves on the Universal ocean of energy.

"Pure freedom, joy, and creativity," Obaa-san continued, "are the intentions of the Universe. A rose, a rainbow, a dolphin, a human being, when broken down to their essential nature, are all expressions of these Universal, life-affirming intentions.

"Of the infinite evolutions of Universal energy, human beings are special. We are unique in our power of consciousness and free will to write our own script, to plot our own course, to direct our own destiny. We have the ability to mold our intentions and desires, to influence the essence of rhythmic energy that flows both inside and outside ourselves."

Obaa-san explained that our intentions are the roots of our desires, and our desires are the sparks of our actions. The more closely we align our intentions with those of the Universe, the more positive and beneficial our actions become. The more we focus our intentions to increase freedom, joy, and creativity for ourselves and others, the more wholly our dreams will be realized. When circumstances in life seem to be moving in the wrong direction, that's a good time to self-reflect and refocus our intentions toward greater freedom, joy, and creativity.

"There are as many methods to focus intention as there are individuals," Obaa-san said. "Some people use prayer or meditation, while others perform various mental and physical exercises. Chanting *Nam-myoho-renge-kyo* each day has helped me master my thoughts, words, and deeds most effectively. Whatever method works best for you, use it to align your actions with your most compassionate intentions. Do so, and you will find everything you need to unlock your deepest happiness, manifest your greatest strengths, and fulfill your noblest wishes. You will have awakened to the power of the Universe within."

God has no religion.

— MAHATMA GANDHI

Have patience with all things, but chiefly with yourself.

Have courage in considering your own imperfections

and instantly set about improving yourself.

Every day begin anew.

— SAINT FRANCIS DE SALES

Wisdom gives rise to courage.

Courage gives rise to compassion.

Compassion gives rise to wisdom.

— DAISAKU IKEDA

CHAPTER SIX

A FIELD OF
POSSIBILITIES

Your life is a fertile field

in which you can plant

any seeds you wish,

creating a harvest of

your own design.

無限の可能性

"Your life is a field of possibilities," Obaa-san continued. "With each of your actions—every thought, word, and deed—you plant new seeds in the fertile ground of your life. Starting today, choose to plant seeds that will grow into your truest dreams. Choose every action wisely, for the harvest you reap will without fail match the seeds you plant."

What Obaa-san spoke of was the concept of karma, or the law of cause and effect. Not unique to the realm of Wabi Sabi, *karma* is an ancient word for "action," meaning that our actions determine our circumstances. "Don't eat too much candy or you'll get an upset stomach," our parents warned us when we were children. After sneaking an extra fistful down our throats, to our surprise we discovered they were right. "Take a sweater when you go out or you'll be cold." "Wash your hands before you eat or you'll get sick." The list goes on.

"Don't stick your finger in an electrical outlet or you'll get a shock" is one warning I will always remember, because I did just that. Feeling daring one day in kindergarten, I actually licked my little finger and stuck it directly in a socket—and, yep, received quite a jolt!

In these ways and countless others, we learn as children about the basic law of causality. As we mature, we come to view cause and effect in an even broader, less immediate way. We've all heard the expressions "You reap what you sow," "Do unto others as you would have done unto you," and "What goes around comes around." As these sayings imply, every thought we think, every word we speak, and every act we carry out generates ripples of Universal energy, producing effects that will return to us in kind. The key to creating the karma we desire, then, is to tailor these effects by choosing wisely among our thoughts, words, and deeds.

To use the imagery of a farm, you and I are essentially growers of infinite possibilities. We are limitless karma farmers who can cultivate whatever we wish. Our lives are the fields, our actions are the seeds, and our circumstances are the harvest.

Whatsoever a man soweth, that shall he also reap.

— GALATIANS 6:7

Good deeds are better than wise sayings.

— TALMUD

When I do good
I feel good.
When I do bad
I feel bad.
And that's my religion.

— ABRAHAM LINCOLN

Ralph Waldo Emerson believed "Thoughts rule the world." And since desires give rise to thoughts, we could also say that "desires rule the world." Our desires guide our entire existences. Even to go on living, for example, we must desire to do so. Our thoughts, words, and deeds, then, are simply expressions of our desires.

"Desires motivate action," Obaa-san said. "Every one of our actions is rooted in this desire or that. By willfully directing our desires, we can choose the exact harvest we wish to reap—joy over sorrow, creativity over habit, free-dom over limitation. When we understand the Universal law of karma in this way, we can't help but feel confident and hopeful. This is the most liberating and empowering knowledge. It reminds us that the flow of destiny is ours to change."

Many of us, unfortunately, don't realize the power we hold over our desires. In time, certain desires repeatedly compel us to perform specific actions, and those actions in turn trigger specific responses from our environment. As we become comfortable with predictable cycles of actions and reactions, we settle into patterns. Herein lies a karma danger zone, for once a pattern of behavior develops, our actions move from the conscious realm into subconscious habits.

The more subconscious habits we allow, the more stagnant our lives become. We may eventually forget why we think, say, and do certain things. All we know is that we have "always" been that way, or perhaps we assume everyone else is that way, too. In such a lazy frame of mind, we relinquish our creative decision-making power. We leave the crucial role of seed planting in the field of our lives to our subconscious habits.

When we give up any part of our lives to a subconscious habit, a piece of our future falls behind us. That is because our subconscious habits are ingrained patterns of behavior, echoes of our past. And since the past can never change, any aspect of our lives controlled by subconscious habits will never change. Stuck in this karmic rut, our past is bound to repeat itself in our future. We can break this cycle only by becoming consciously aware of the decisions we make at every moment.

"The most regrettable thing about subconscious decision-making," Obaa-san said, "is that many of us don't even realize we have a choice. Every action is a choice—everything we think, say, or do is preceded by a *decision* about what to think, say, or do. When we abandon this process to our subconscious minds, we often don't realize we have a choice; yet we always do. There is not the slightest need to think, speak, or behave as we have before. Starting this instant, we can take control of our karma and direct our lives toward greater happiness by making decisions with careful awareness."

Obaa-san knew how easy it is to slip into patterns of repetitive behavior and decision making. Throughout her life as a Tea Master, she had repeated the same actions countless times during highly choreographed and regimented ceremonies. Instead of allowing such predictability to create subconscious habits, however, Obaa-san used those experiences as training. No matter how many times before she had repeated the exact same actions, she always maintained her present-moment awareness, making a conscious decision to do so each and every time.

Today, my dog Athena reminds me of the common tendency to create subconscious habits. When she was a puppy, I didn't know how to cook very well. Every time I opened the oven door, a piercing scream from the smoke alarm followed, sending Athena running outdoors in terror (with an earache, I'm sure). Although my domestic skills have improved and I haven't set off an alarm in a long while, now Athena only needs to hear the oven door open to go flying out the dog door. She has subconsciously connected the two events (me cooking and alarms screaming), so her response is the same even when only one event occurs.

How many of us are like Athena? We become so conditioned to familiar people, places, and events that we don't truly see situations as they are. We lose our present-moment awareness, and our responses become automatic. When our reactions become subconscious and reflexive, we have forgotten that each and every one of our responses is still a decision.

Our deeds are seeds of fate, sown here on earth,
but bringing forth their harvest in eternity.

— GEORGE DANA BOARDMAN

Increase your joy by actively doing
the good you wish to have done to you.
Decrease your suffering by refusing to do
the bad that has been done to you.

— DAISAKU IKEDA

When one commits an act,
one becomes the heir to that act.

— SHAKYAMUNI

"If I were to give you a gift," Obaa-san said, "most likely you would make the decision to be delighted. If, however, I were to take something you cherish, you would likely make the decision to be distressed. On the surface, these reactions may not seem like decisions, but they are. You can decide to be undisturbed by the loss of a possession— after all, you know that nothing lasts forever, and as the old adage goes, 'Whatever you have lost has simply returned from whence it came.' On the flip side, you can also decide not to let a gift influence you one way or another.

"By consciously controlling our moment-to-moment decisions, we become the masters of our actions," Obaa-san said. "As the masters of our actions, we become the masters of our destiny."

Obaa-san was a living example of this principle. I remember shopping one Sunday with her at an open-air market in the city. A few angry-looking men from what appeared to be a biker gang were making a loud fuss over something with a local shopkeeper. As Obaa-san and I walked by the scene, one of the men whirled around to leave, yelling profanities, and carelessly bumped into Obaa-san. Losing his balance, he tripped against a towering display of wooden boxes that crashed down around him.

Adding to his humiliation and anger, the man barked a few rough words at Obaa-san as if she were to blame. Obaa-san calmly replied, "Excuse me, sir." Fumbling to get up and impervious to Obaa-san's politeness, the man stormed off, grumbling in frustration. As we watched his self-imposed drama march away with him, Obaa-san bowed low in his direction and quietly said, "Thank you very much." Her tone, to my surprise, was respectful and sincere.

To be honest, when that ranting man bumped into my grandma and yelled obscenities, my initial reaction was to pound him a good one right on his big, dumb head! At the very least, I wanted to let out a few choice words.

Thanks to Obaa-san's good example, however, I avoided any foolhardy actions.

After we helped the shopkeeper clean up the mess, we enjoyed the remainder of our day in the city. At home that night, I asked Obaa-san why she had softly said "thank you" as that stranger stormed away. How could she even have been thinking "thank you" after someone bumped into her and yelled obscenities at her?

"I said 'thank you' as a little prayer of appreciation to that suffering man, to myself, to the Universe, for giving me an opportunity to change a bit of my karma," Obaa-san explained. "Who knows how or why, but my karma led me to be involved in those unpleasant circumstances today. I could have decided to be insulted or angry, but I wanted that karmic scene to be finished. I wanted it to end there and never come back to me again. So I decided to break the cycle by accepting responsibility for my role in it and say 'thank you' for a chance to clear my karmic slate."

As I paused to consider her comments, Obaa-san asked me, "What would you have done if that same scenario had happened to you?"

"I think I would have at least said something rude to that man."

"Why would you be rude to him?"

"Because he was rude to me first!" I answered.

"Actually, if you consider it deeply," she said, "I believe you will realize the reason you would be rude is that you are accustomed to being rude in such situations. You are used to reacting to people in the same way they treat you. When someone is generous with you, you respond with pleasure. When someone is rude to you, it seems natural to be rude in return. It has become your habit. But it doesn't need to be—you still have a choice. Think how people would react if, when they were rude to you, you responded with compassion, or when they were thoughtless and self-centered, you were kind. Remember, it has less to do with others and more to do with you. You are the one planting karmic seeds in your life, after all, and no one else."

Whether we like it or not, the circumstances we are experiencing today are the results of actions we've taken in the past. We may not fathom the reason, but the fact is that Obaa-san carried the karma to be mistreated that day. If she had mistreated anyone else in return, she would have again created the karma to be mistreated herself. If she had reacted to abuse with more abuse, she would have strengthened the cycle, planting more seeds of turmoil in her life to be harvested in the future.

In this and every moment, we have a choice to plant the seeds we wish to harvest. We can increase our joy by actively doing the good we wish to have returned to us. We can decrease our suffering by refusing to return the bad that has been done to us. Our lives are fertile fields of infinite possibilities.

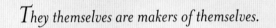

They themselves are makers of themselves.

—JAMES ALLEN

People are like stained glass windows.
  They sparkle and shine when the sun is out,
but when the darkness sets in, their true beauty
    is revealed only by the light from within.

—ELISABETH KÜBLER-ROSS

The lotus flower blooms most beautifully

from the deepest and thickest mud.

— BUDDHIST PROVERB

CHAPTER SEVEN

THE TRUE
BEAUTY OF
YOUR LIFE

Appreciate this and every moment
no matter how imperfect,
for this moment is your life.

真の美しさ

*B*lue tile roofs and lush countryside flashed by my window in the Hikari bullet train as Obaa-san and I made our way to the airport for my flight home. By this time the next day, I'd be surfing with my friends back in Del Mar, wondering if my Kyoto adventure was only a dream.

As we glided out of the train station and gracefully cruised to a speed of 170 miles per hour, the Hikari's hypnotic hum lulled everyone to silence. It was always like that on the bullet train, as if the sheer force of speed mesmerized travelers into quiet contemplation.

I thought about the events that had brought me to Japan and was amazed at how much I had learned in just one summer. Only weeks earlier, I was still reeling from the death of my father. He was just shy of his forty-fifth birthday, and I was only fourteen when suddenly he was gone. Getting a sense of mortality at such a young age was like hearing a crash of thunder, waking me from a living sleep, reminding me in no uncertain terms to appreciate the little things, the incremental experiences, the steady flow of moments that make up a lifetime. When you boil it down, that's what a lifetime really is—a rolling stream of moments, some shining bright, some darker than others.

The importance of this awakening became more obvious as I opened my heart to the lessons of Wabi Sabi. Somewhere along the way, a light came on with a clear message for me: Appreciate this and every moment, no matter how imperfect, for this moment is your life. When you reject this moment, you reject your life. You don't have to settle for this moment, you are free to steer a different course, but for now this moment is yours, so be mindful to make the most of it.

Take a deep breath, smile, be yourself. Life is too important to be spent any other way.

As I shared these thoughts with Obaa-san, she knowingly nodded. "Tuck that little piece of enlightenment in your sleeve and keep it close. When you add it to everything else you have learned, it will help you shine. Like a diamond in the making, the more heat and pressure you face, the more brilliant you will grow."

We felt the Hikari begin to slow, and the flashing blur outside the train windows gradually took on the shapes of trees and buildings again. As we arrived at my point of departure, Obaa-san drew from her purse a surprise. It was a fine hand-tooled journal, resembling her own. "Next time you come to Kyoto, I hope to see it filled with pearls of wisdom," she said.

"It will be," I promised, as I tucked it in my backpack and we bid each other farewell.

Flying over the Pacific that night, I watched the moonlit

vastness of the water below and considered those three words from Obaa-san: "pearls of wisdom." What a fitting expression, I thought. A perfect example of living Wabi Sabi. When imperfection exists in the body (the life) of an oyster, sediment that just can't be removed, the oyster bathes it with layers of soothing coating, crafting it into a pearl. The oyster transforms potentially worthless, damaging, and unchangeable imperfections into treasures of value and beauty. Now that's what I call wisdom.

*M*ore valuable than treasures in a storehouse

are the treasures of the body,

and the treasures of the heart

are the most valuable of all.

— Nichiren

*M*other Nature makes no mistakes.

— Tsunesaburo Makiguchi

Breaking me from my thoughts, the cheerful little girl sitting next to me asked if I'd like to see her book of fairy tales. As she proudly explained to me the colorful illustrations from her favorite stories, I realized that the heroes and heroines in those stories, and in virtually all children's stories, share a common characteristic—flaws, and sometimes major ones.

Think of the characters in *The Wizard of Oz, The Lion King, The Ugly Duckling, Beauty and the Beast, Finding Nemo*—and the list goes on. Our favorite imperfect characters share the same way of finding their happy endings: by realizing that who they have always wanted to be, they already are.

Perhaps we embrace these timeless characters because in our hearts our greatest wish, too, is simply to be ourselves. It sounds like the easiest thing in the world, to be ourselves. But it is not.

Why? Because we've spent a lifetime listening to people tell us that being ourselves just isn't good enough. We're too young, too old, too short, too tall, too gay, too straight, too black, too white, too thin, too fat, too this, too that. Reacting to these messages, many of us try to mold superficial pictures of ourselves—our appearance, our behavior, our possessions—to the form we think others will find acceptable. Yet our most meaningful accomplishments happen deep within ourselves, in heartfelt places others can see only through the glimmer in our eyes.

If you're like me, your greatest bliss has come when you least expected it; not through material achievements but through your openhearted humanity. At a battered women's shelter in California, I served as a children's counselor. In Japan, I worked as a model. I'm proud of all my accomplishments, but the satisfaction of seeing my image plastered across Asia was nothing compared with the reward of teaching a neglected five-year-old boy to tie his shoelaces. Witnessing his usually lackluster little face light up with pride was a perfect moment in a most imperfect place—a sublime experience engraved as a treasure of my heart.

I once wondered why small, obscure, unseen events like this could touch our hearts so profoundly. I now realize that it's because such Wabi Sabi moments open doors to the self-acceptance we all crave. That little boy felt as mighty as if I had helped him defeat a giant. In reality, what I gave him was insignificant compared with what he unwittingly gave me.

When we encounter weaknesses or imperfections in another, the wisdom of Wabi Sabi allows us to see a reflection of our own hidden vulnerabilities. And when we help others look beyond their imperfections with confidence and clarity, we discover that we can do the same for ourselves.

Most of us, I believe, want to increase the good in our lives without having to become impossibly perfect people or change the entire arrangement of our imperfect lifestyles. We don't want to move to a monastery or stop eating our favorite foods. What we really want is to know happiness here and now, in the midst of this imperfect world, just as we are.

If there is one thing the wisdom of Wabi Sabi shows us, it is that we *can* know this kind of joy, right now, as is. It reminds us that no matter what our circumstances, if we always strive to be joyful here and now, then we will forever be joyful, because there is only here and now. It teaches us to do what the oysters do, create value from life's sediment, the imperfections that could otherwise block our potential.

We all have misfit aspects of our lives, the "strangers within," waiting to be cultivated into pearls of wisdom. We can make this transformation once we accept ourselves unconditionally. This does not mean ignoring our faults or making excuses for them or never trying to improve ourselves.

On the contrary, it means doing everything we can to improve ourselves based on the conviction that our unique flaws are the raw materials of our unique treasures and strengths. It means nurturing new patterns of thought and action, taking charge of our feelings and responses, and finding joy in the face of adversity. It means being ourselves and living true to our hearts, flaws and all.

That's what this book is all about. That's what living Wabi Sabi is all about.

Recently, as I chanted *Nam-myoho-renge-kyo* with the dawning sun, the way I have every day since that life-changing summer in Kyoto, I wondered what more I could write to sum up the essence of living Wabi Sabi, to gracefully draw this imperfect little book to a "perfect" close.

Opening the journal Obaa-san gave me so long ago, I rediscovered the answer—an inscription from her that captures it all:

Living Wabi Sabi,

complete within

that which is incomplete,

forever revealing

the true beauty of your life.

ACKNOWLEDGMENTS

Supporting the success of this and all my books is a team of world-class creative collaborators and loving friends and family. I especially owe gratitude to Jennifer Fox, my star editor at Andrews McMeel Publishing; Sheree Bykofsky, my steadfast friend and agent; Matthew Taylor, for his genius artistry; Holly Camerlinck, Laura Shaw, Julie Barnes, Lisa Martin, and Lee Fukui, for their magnificent design work; Lisa Carter Kirk and Laurie Viera Rigler, for illuminating my literary path; Wendell Brown, for a winning and happy partnership in life; Princess, for being the embodiment of joy every moment; and of course, Obaa-san, whose wisdom, courage, and compassion continue to inspire and uplift me every day.